AF557765

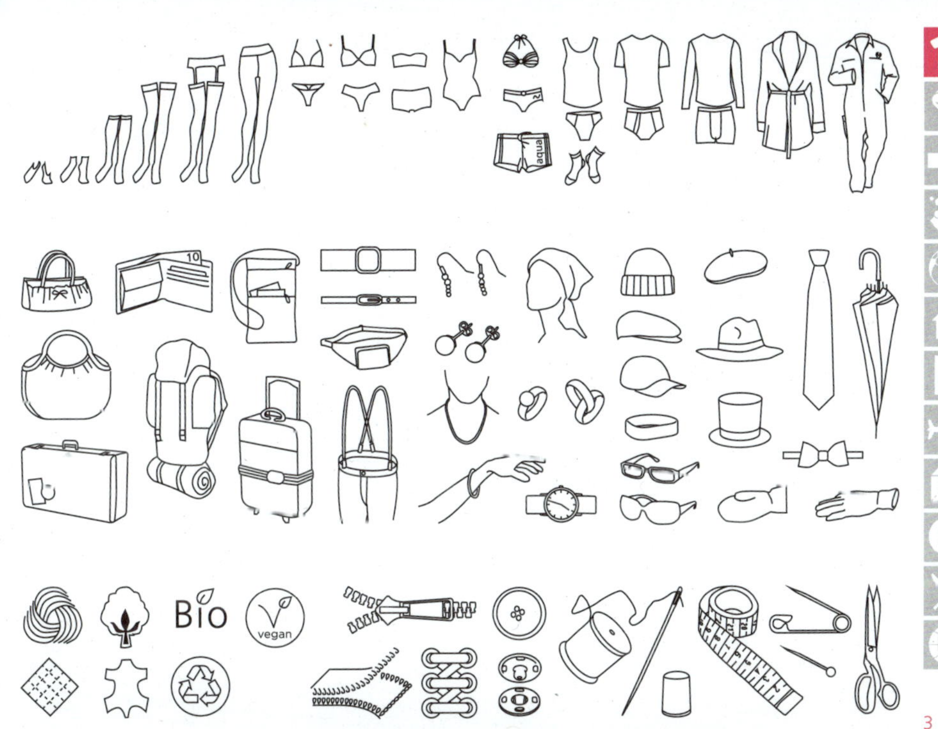
aqua
10
Bio
vegan

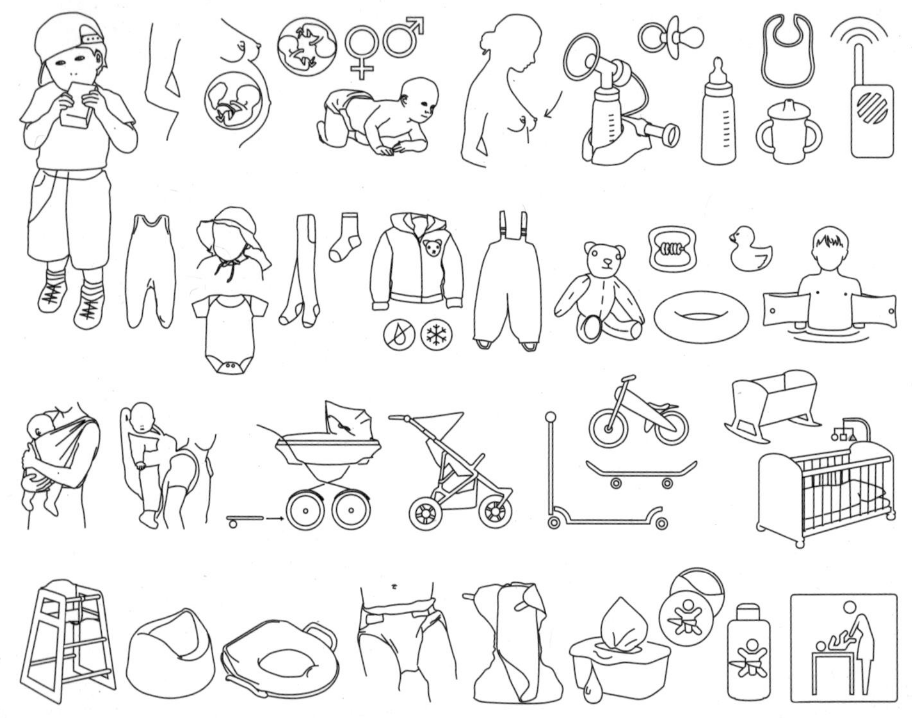

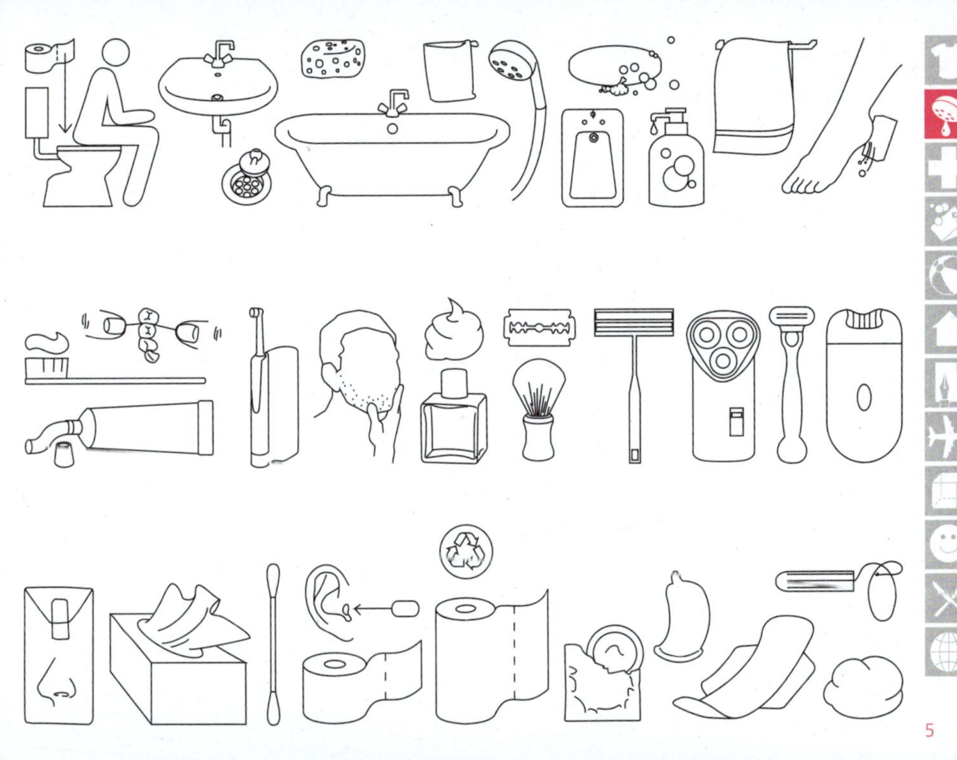

vegan
15
max. 1liter
max. 100 ml

POLICE
C
Xi
N
T
E
F+

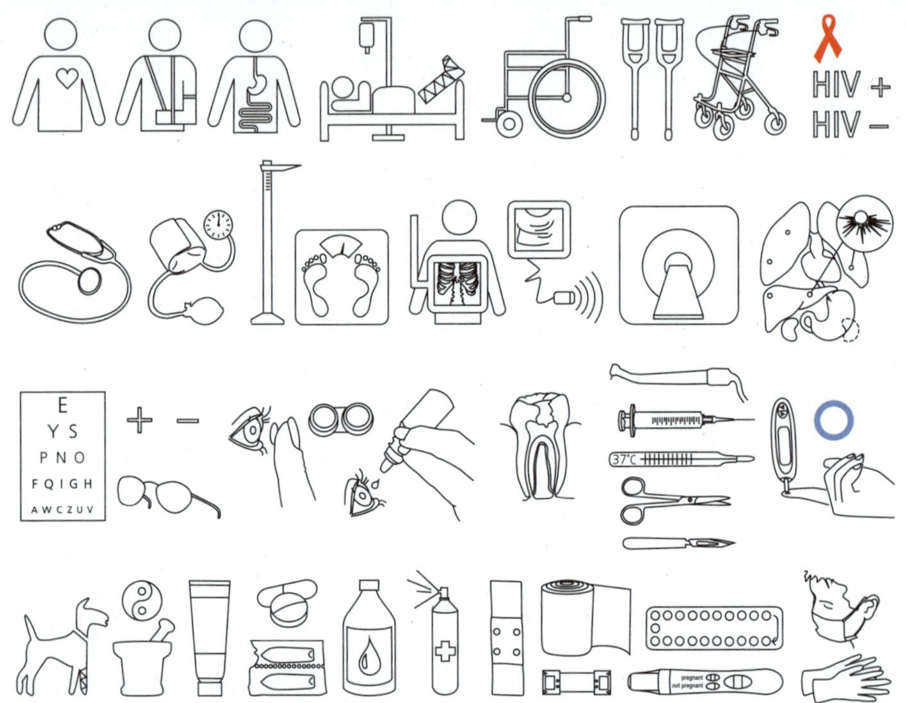
HIV +
HIV –
E
Y S
P N O
F Q I G H
A W C Z U V
37°C
pregnant
not pregnant

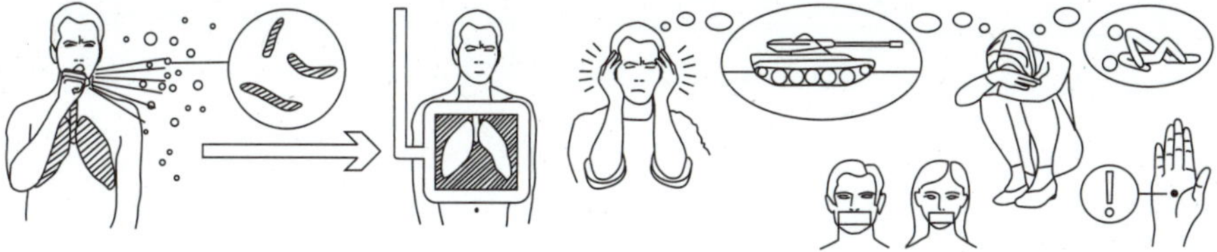

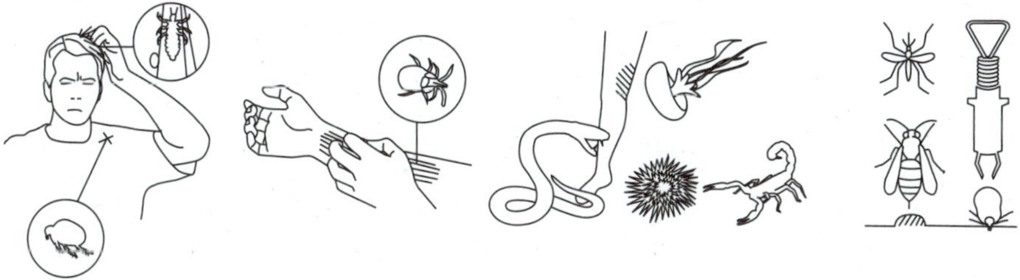

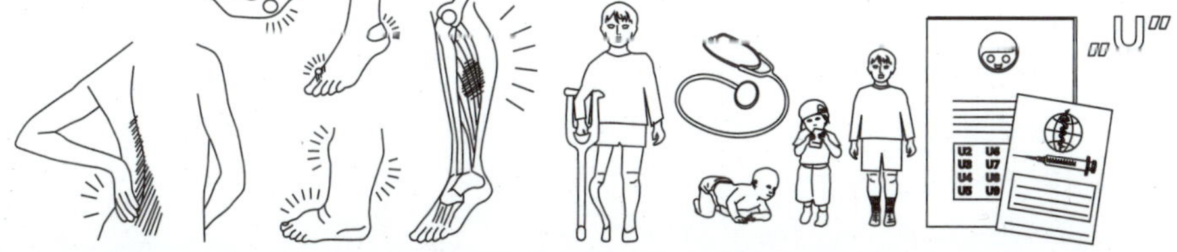
„U"
U2 U6
U3 U7
U4 U8
U5 U9

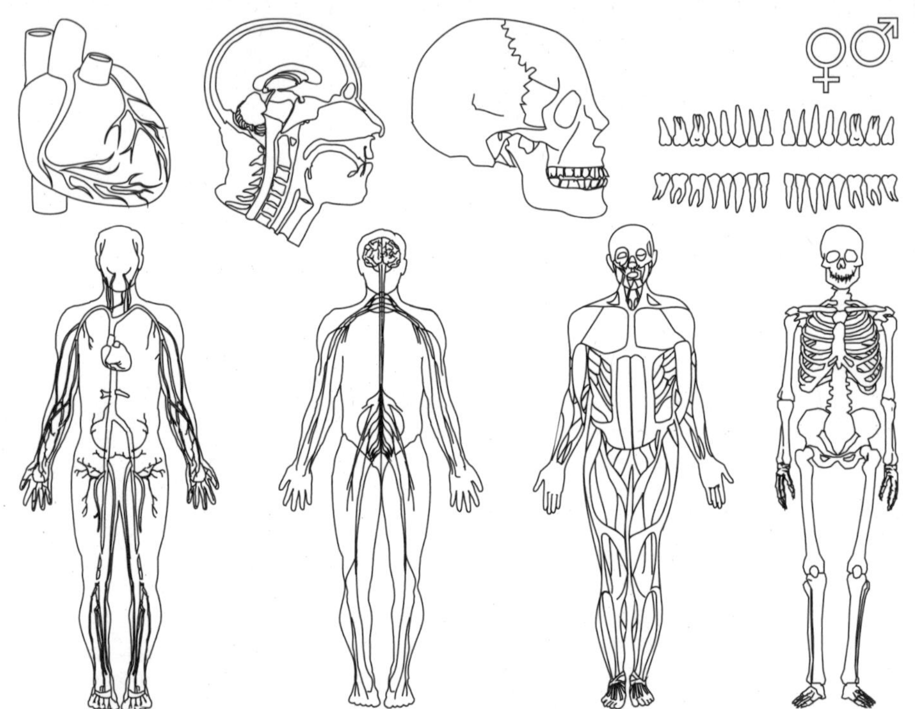

0 1 2 3 4 5 6 7 8 9 10

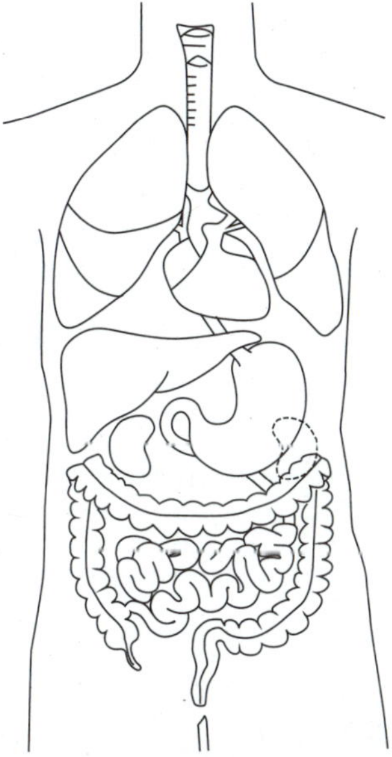

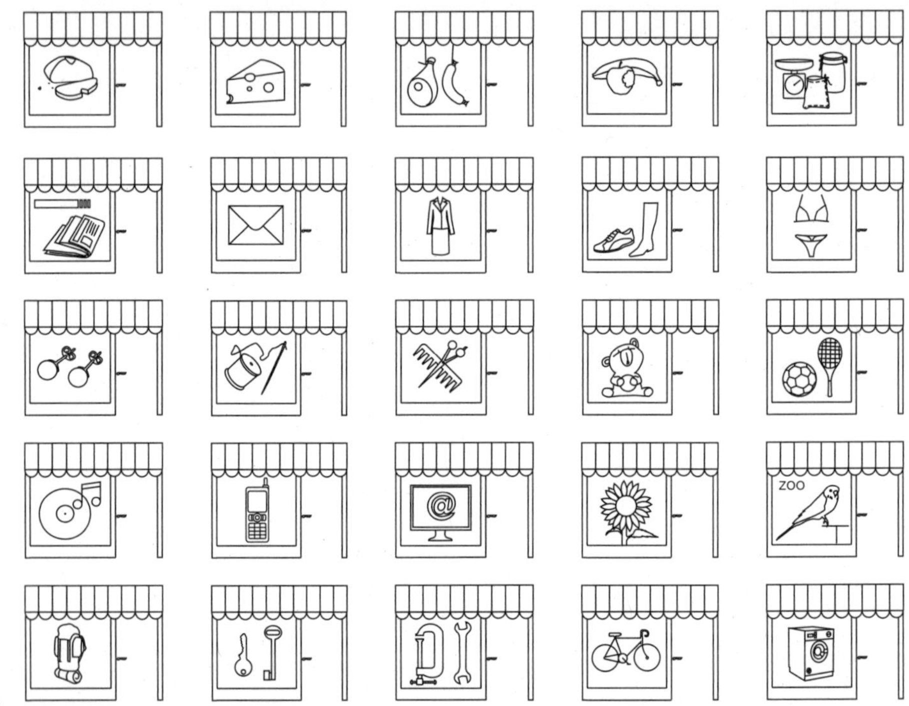
ZOO

BANK
10
10
10
10
10
50
TRAVELLER CHEQUE
ATM
BANK
12
3
6
9
super
moda

@
MENU
MENU
WC
23,00
1.
2.
3.

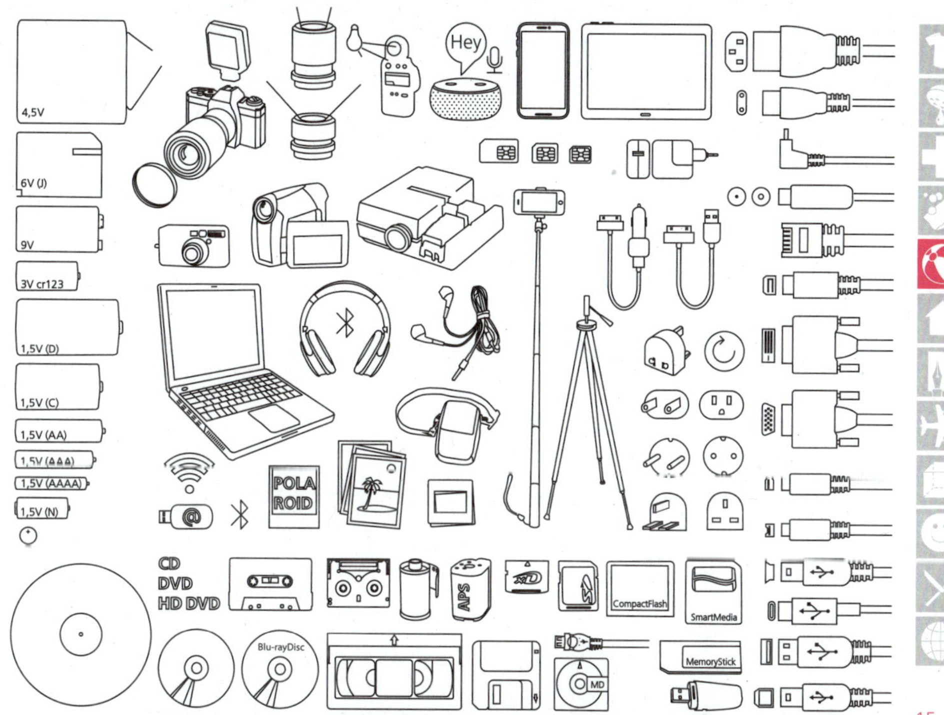
4,5V
6V (J)
9V
3V cr123
1,5V (D)
1,5V (C)
1,5V (AA)
1,5V (AAA)
1,5V (AAAA)
1,5V (N)
Hey
POLA ROID
CD
DVD
HD DVD
APS
CompactFlash
SmartMedia
Blu-rayDisc
MD
MemoryStick

18m

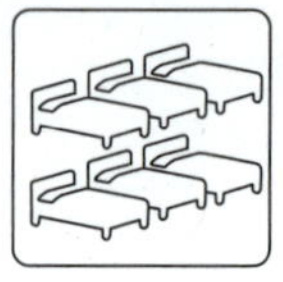
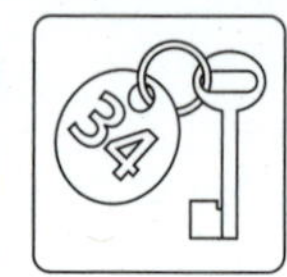
34

HOSTELLING
INTERNATIONAL

P

@

WC

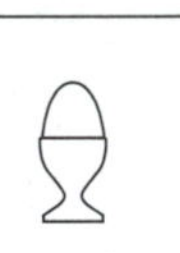

ZZZ!!!

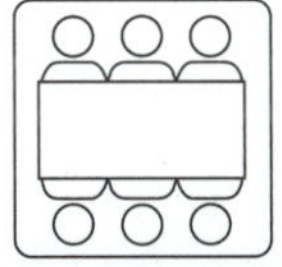

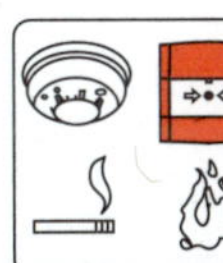

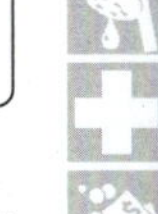

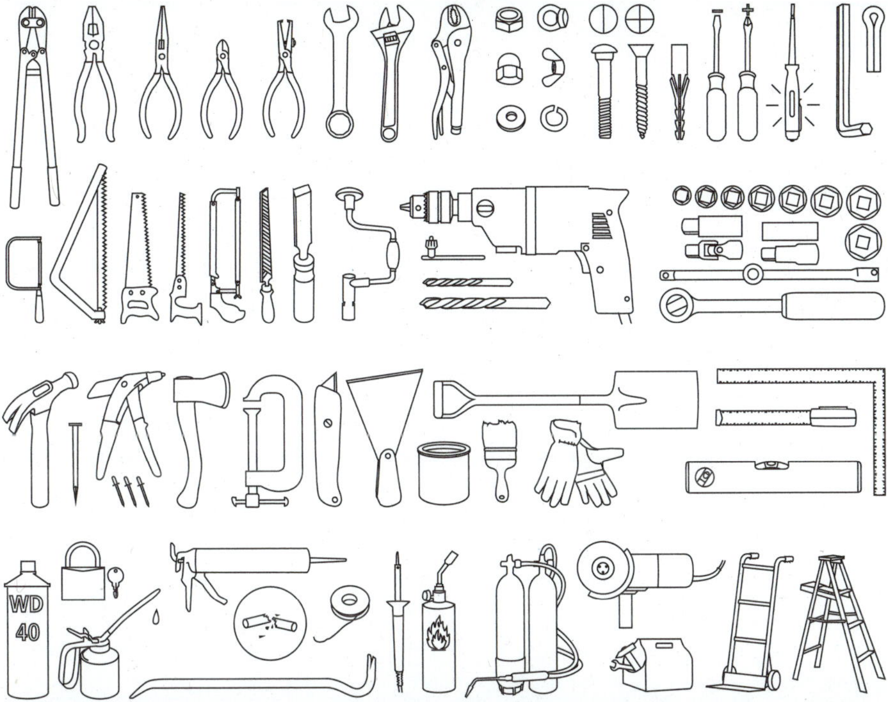

WD
40

ZOLL
DOUANE
EMBASSY
OF
REPUBLIC
VISA
§
@
50
1.
1.1.
1.2.
2.
FAX

A B
A B
I./II./III.
1./2./3.
M
H

TAXI

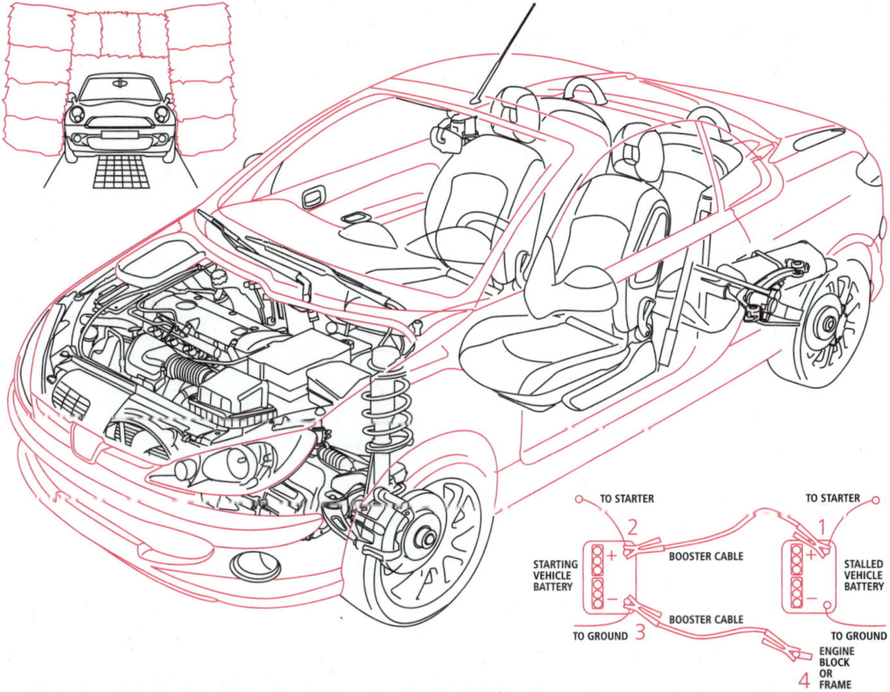

TO STARTER
2
STARTING VEHICLE BATTERY
BOOSTER CABLE
TO STARTER
1
STALLED VEHICLE BATTERY
BOOSTER CABLE
TO GROUND 3
TO GROUND
4 ENGINE BLOCK OR FRAME

D
N
P
A10
100
↑↑
↗70
11:15
3:00h
B -1342
91
Pb
LPG Gas
95
Pb
D
98
D
1:50
VIGNETTE

Street
ABC
3 km
2 km
5 km
N
W
E
S
50?
A
B

City
Guide

VOTE
EMBASSY OF REPUBLIC
VISA

DEPTH
30.5
METERS
SPEED
15.3
KNOTS
112,5°
225°
135°
112,5°

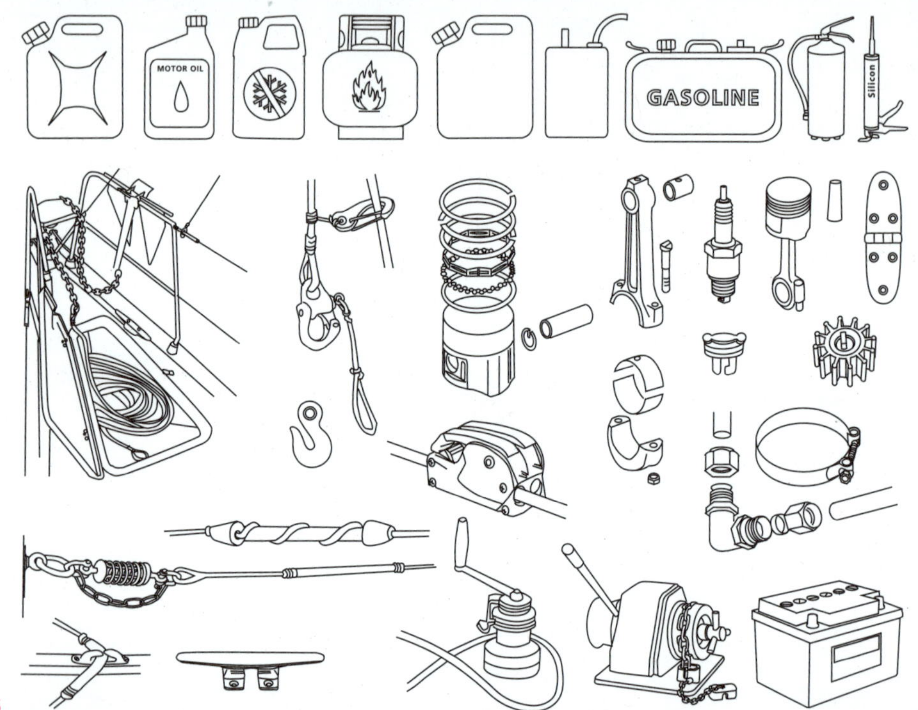
MOTOR OIL
GASOLINE
Silicon

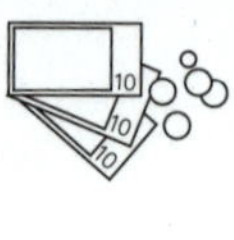

€ $ US$ ¢ £ ¥ kr CNY sFr

R RUR NIS ½ ¼ ¾ ‰ %

kJ Watt Volt kWh PS db

1cm	0,4 inch
1inch	2,54 cm
1m	3,3 ft
1ft	0,3 m
1km	0,6 mile
1mile	1,6 km

30 km/h	19 mph
70 km/h	43 mph
120 km/h	74 mph
30 mph	48 km/h
70 mph	113 km/h
120 mph	193 km/h

$1 m^2$	10,76 sq ft
1 sq ft	$0,1 m^2$
1ha	2,5 acre
1acre	0,4 ha
$1 km^2$	0,4 sq mi
1sq mi	$2,6 km^2$

1ml	0,03 fl oz
1fl oz	28 ml
1liter	0,26 gallon
1gallon	3,8 liter

1g	0,03 oz
1oz	28,35 g
1kg	2,2 lbs
1lbs	0,45 kg

1 2 3 4 5 6 7 8 9 10

I II III IV V VI VII VIII IX X

١ ٢ ٣ ٤ ٥ ٦ ٧ ٨ ٩ ١٠

0 10 100 1,000 10,000 100,000 1,000,000 10,000,000

1 2 3 4 5 6 7 8 9 10 11 12 13 14 15 16 17 18 19 20 21 22 23 24 25 26 27 28 29 30 31 32 33 34 35
36 37 38 39 40 41 42 43 44 45 46 47 48 49 50 51 52 53 54 55 56 57 58 59 60 61 62 63 64 65 66 67 68
69 70 71 72 73 74 75 76 77 78 79 80 81 82 83 84 85 86 87 88 89 90 91 92 93 94 95 96 97 98 99 100

inch ½ 1 1½ 2 2½ 3 3½ 4 4½ 5

cm 1 2 3 4 5 6 7 8 9 10 11 12 13

ZZZ

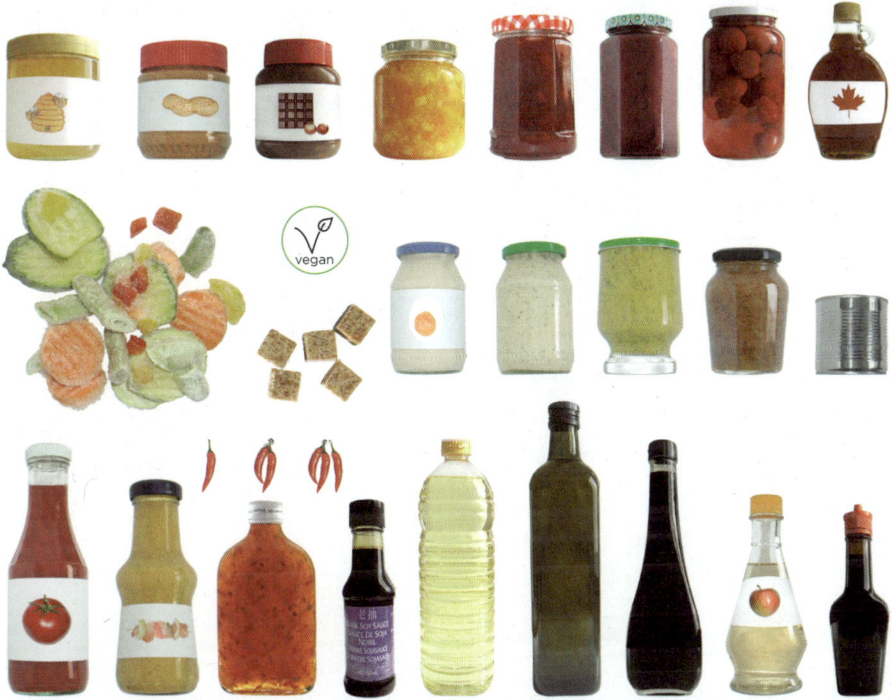
vegan
老抽
Soy Sauce
Noire

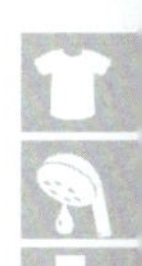

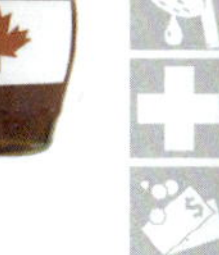

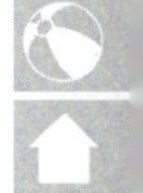

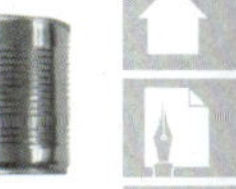

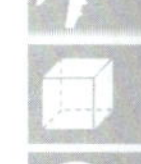

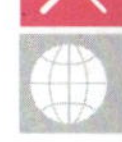

-L

Bio

حلال
HALAL

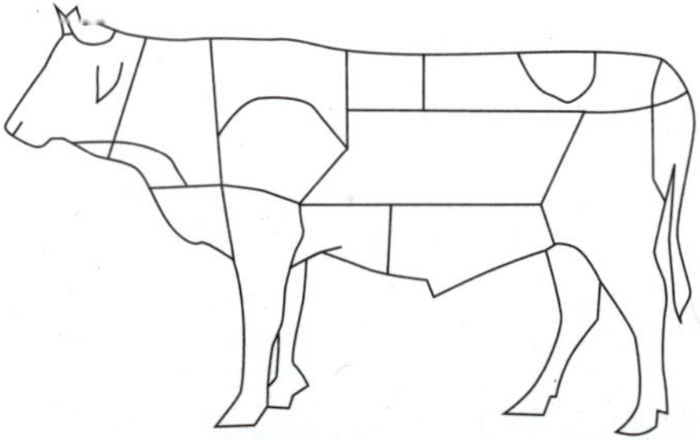

H2O
H2O
H2O
3,5%
1,5%
0,2%
-L
12%
Soy Milk
Cola
ENERGY
KAKAO
%
%
WINE
WINE
VODKA
GRAPPA
TEQUILA
RUM
GIN
WHISKY
SAKE

vegan
Bio
حلال
HALAL

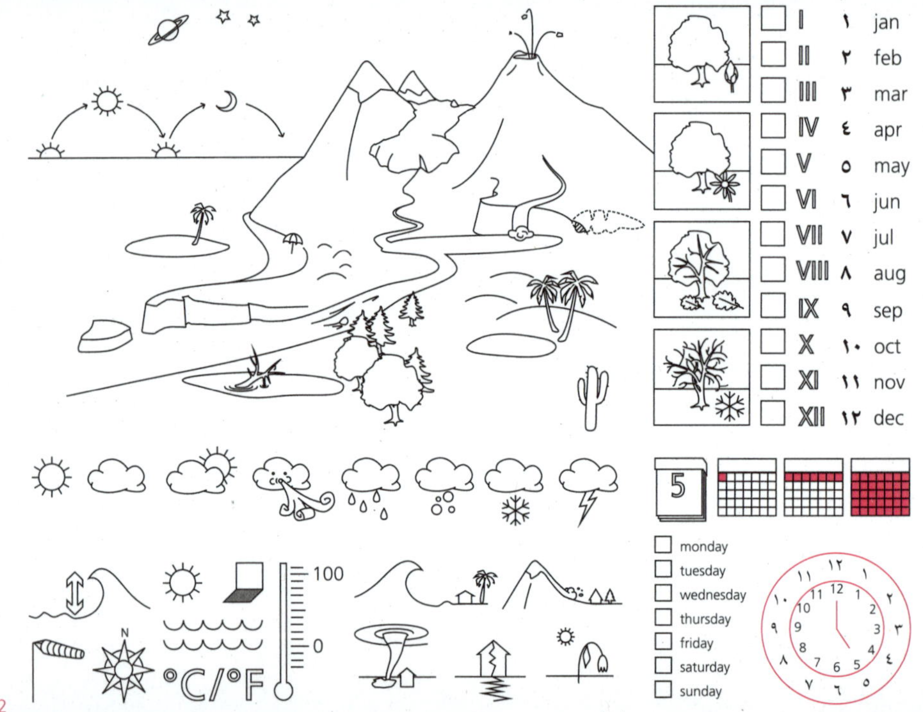
I ١ jan
II ٢ feb
III ٣ mar
IV ٤ apr
V ٥ may
VI ٦ jun
VII ٧ jul
VIII ٨ aug
IX ٩ sep
X ١٠ oct
XI ١١ nov
XII ١٢ dec
5
100
0
N
°C/°F
monday
tuesday
wednesday
thursday
friday
saturday
sunday
١٢ ١ ٢ ٣ ٤ ٥ ٦ ٧ ٨ ٩ ١٠ ١١
12 1 2 3 4 5 6 7 8 9 10 11

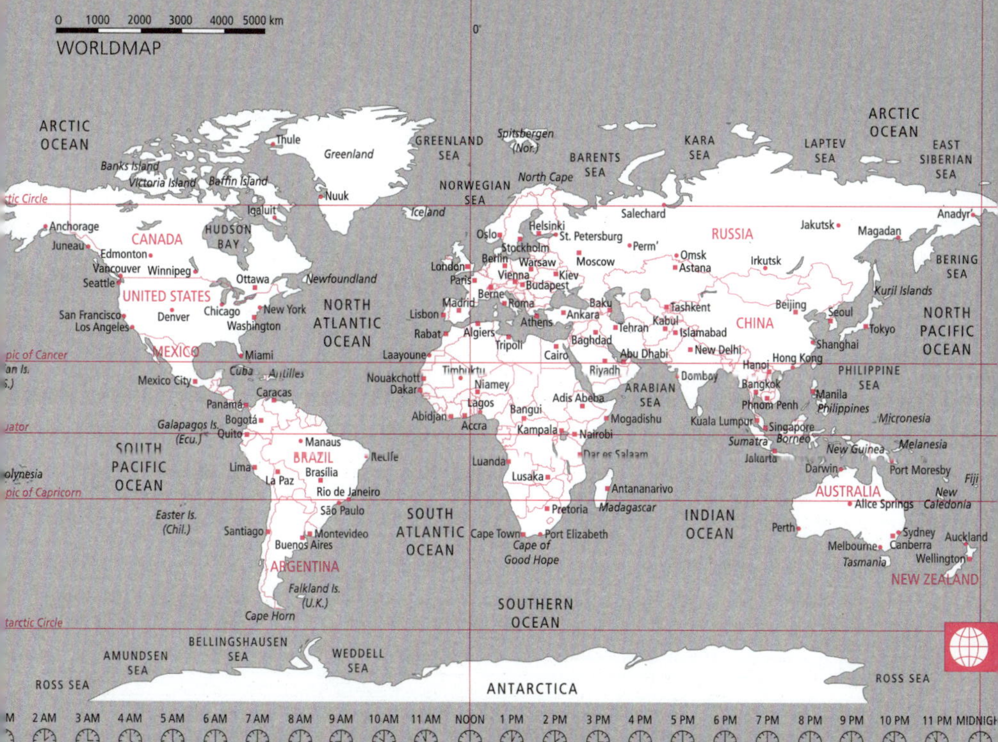

0 1000 2000 3000 4000 5000 km
WORLDMAP
0°
ARCTIC OCEAN
Banks Island
Victoria Island
Baffin Island
Thule
Greenland
GREENLAND SEA
Spitsbergen (Nor.)
BARENTS SEA
KARA SEA
LAPTEV SEA
ARCTIC OCEAN
EAST SIBERIAN SEA
North Cape
NORWEGIAN SEA
Nuuk
Iqaluit
Iceland
Salechard
Anadyr'
Anchorage
Juneau
CANADA
HUDSON BAY
Edmonton
Vancouver
Winnipeg
Seattle
Ottawa
Newfoundland
UNITED STATES
San Francisco
Los Angeles
Denver
Chicago
New York
Washington
NORTH ATLANTIC OCEAN
MEXICO
Miami
Cuba
Antilles
Mexico City
Caracas
Panamá
Bogotá
Galapagos Is. (Ecu.)
Quito
SOUTH PACIFIC OCEAN
Manaus
BRAZIL
Recife
Lima
La Paz
Brasília
Rio de Janeiro
São Paulo
Easter Is. (Chil.)
Santiago
Montevideo
Buenos Aires
ARGENTINA
Falkland Is. (U.K.)
Cape Horn
Oslo
Helsinki
St. Petersburg
Stockholm
London
Berlin
Warsaw
Moscow
Paris
Vienna
Kiev
Budapest
Berne
Madrid
Roma
Lisbon
Rabat
Algiers
Tripoli
Athens
Ankara
Baku
Laayoune
Cairo
Baghdad
Tehran
Riyadh
Abu Dhabi
Nouakchott
Dakar
Timbuktu
Niamey
Lagos
Abidjan
Accra
Bangui
Adis Abeba
Mogadishu
Kampala
Nairobi
Dar es Salaam
Luanda
Lusaka
Antananarivo
Madagascar
Pretoria
Cape Town
Port Elizabeth
Cape of Good Hope
SOUTH ATLANTIC OCEAN
ARABIAN SEA
RUSSIA
Perm'
Omsk
Astana
Irkutsk
Jakutsk
Magadan
BERING SEA
Kuril Islands
Tashkent
Kabul
Islamabad
New Delhi
CHINA
Beijing
Seoul
Tokyo
Shanghai
Hong Kong
Hanoi
Bombay
Bangkok
Phnom Penh
Manila
Philippines
PHILIPPINE SEA
NORTH PACIFIC OCEAN
Micronesia
Kuala Lumpur
Singapore
Sumatra
Borneo
Jakarta
New Guinea
Melanesia
Darwin
Port Moresby
Fiji
AUSTRALIA
Alice Springs
New Caledonia
Perth
INDIAN OCEAN
Sydney
Canberra
Melbourne
Tasmania
Auckland
Wellington
NEW ZEALAND
SOUTHERN OCEAN
AMUNDSEN SEA
BELLINGSHAUSEN SEA
WEDDELL SEA
ROSS SEA
ANTARCTICA
ROSS SEA
2 AM
3 AM
4 AM
5 AM
6 AM
7 AM
8 AM
9 AM
10 AM
11 AM
NOON
1 PM
2 PM
3 PM
4 PM
5 PM
6 PM
7 PM
8 PM
9 PM
10 PM
11 PM

NORTH AMERICA
0 500 1000 1500 km
ARCTIC OCEAN
PACIFIC OCEAN
ATLANTIC OCEAN
BEAUFORT SEA
BAFFIN BAY
DAVIS STRAIT
LABRADOR SEA
HUDSON BAY
GULF OF ALASKA
GULF OF MEXICO
CARIBBEAN SEA
RUSSIA
ICELAND
CANADA
UNITED STATES
MEXICO
BAHAMAS
CUBA
HAITI
DOM. REP.
JAMAICA
BELIZE
GUATEM.
HONDURAS
EL SALV.
NICARAGUA
COSTA RICA
PANAMA
COLOMBIA
Pewek
Anadyr'
Providenija
Point Hope
Barrow
Kotzebue
Alaska (U.S.)
Bethel
Tanana
Fairbanks
Platinum
Kenai
Anchorage
Cordova
Kodiak
Juneau
Sitka
Queen Charlotte Islands
Hawaii
Greenland
Ellesmere Island
Melville Island
Devon Island
Banks Island
Victoria Island
Baffin Island
Southampton Island
Newfoundland
Isla Guadalupe (Mex.)
Upernavik
Angmagssalik
Godthåb
Tununirusiq
Iqaluit
Naujaat
Inuvik
Great Bear Lake
Great Slave Lake
Lake Winnipeg
Lake Superior
Lake Michigan
Ft. Good Hope
Whitehorse
Ft. Simpson
Hay River
Ft. Nelson
Qamani 'tuaq
Ft. Chipewyan
Churchill
Dawson Creek
Ft. Mc Murray
Prince George
Edmonton
Calgary
Saskatoon
Vancouver
Victoria
Regina
Lethbridge
Winnipeg
Thunder Bay
Kuujjuaq
Nain
Happy Valley-Goose Bay
Schefferville
Chisasibi
Chicoutimi
Moosonee
Québec
Halifax
Sudbury
Montreal
Ottawa
Toronto
Tacoma
Seattle
Portland
Spokane
Helena
Minot
Salem
Butte
Billings
Fargo
Eugene
Boise
Pierre
Minneapolis
Pocatello
Milwaukee
Detroit
Buffalo
Cleveland
Concord
Boston
New York
Philadelphia
Washington
Richmond
Ogden
Salt Lake City
Cheyenne
Omaha
Des Moines
Chicago
Pittsburgh
Indianapolis
Sacramento
Reno
San Francisco
San Jose
Fresno
Las Vegas
Denver
Kansas City
Missouri
St. Louis
Louisville
Ohio
Colorado
Pueblo
Wichita
Oklahoma City
Memphis
Mississippi
Nashville
Charlotte
Los Angeles
San Diego
Tijuana
Mexicali
Albuquerque
Amarillo
Red
Atlanta
Charleston
Birmingham
Phoenix
Tucson
El Paso
Ciudad Juárez
Fort Worth
Dallas
Baton Rouge
Mobile
Jacksonville
New Orleans
Austin
Houston
Rio Grande
Tampa
Miami
Nassau
Hermosillo
Ciudad Obregón
Corpus Christi
Culiacán
Torreón
Monterrey
La Habana
Santa Clara
Santo Domingo
Durango
San José del Cabo
San Luis Potosi
Tampico
Port-au-Prince
Mérida
Kingston
Guadalajara
Morelia
Mexico City
Veracruz
Belize City
Acapulco
Oaxaca
Guatemala
Tegucigalpa
Barranquilla
Cartagena
Managua
San José
Panamá
Medellín
Santa Fe de Bogotá
Cali
Neiva
Tumaco

SOUTH AMERICA
0 500 1000 1500 km
ATLANTIC OCEAN
PACIFIC OCEAN
CARIBBEAN SEA
ATLANTIC OCEAN
MEXICO
CUBA
La Habana
Santa Clara
Cienfuegos
Turks and Caicos-Is. (U.K.)
Cayman-Is. (U.K.)
HAITI
DOM.REP.
Port-au-Prince
Santo Domingo
Puerto Rico (U.S.)
British Virgin Is. (U.K.)
JAMAICA
Kingston
ANTIGUA & BARBUDA
Guadeloupe (Fr.)
DOMINICA
Martinique (Fr.)
ST.LUCIA
St. Vincent
BARBADOS
GRENADA
TRINIDAD & TOBAGO
HONDURAS
Tegucigalpa
NICARAGUA
Managua
COSTA RICA
San José
PANAMA
Panamá
Aruba (Neth.)
Netherlands Antilles
Barranquilla
Cartagena
Montería
Maracaibo
Caracas
Barquisimeto
Cúcuta
San Cristóbal
Ciudad Bolívar
Medellín
Bucaramanga
VENEZUELA
GUYANA
Georgetown
Paramaribo
SURINAME
Cayenne
FRENCH GUIANA
Armenia
Santa Fe de Bogotá
Buenaventura
Cali
COLOMBIA
Boa Vista
Popayán
Pasto
Esmeraldas
Mitú
Negro
Japurá
Macapá
Barcelos
Belém
Quito
ECUADOR
Riobamba
Galapagos Is. (Ecu.)
Guayaquil
Cuenca
Iquitos
Amazonas
Tefé
Manaus
Santarém
São Luís
Parnaíba
Fortaleza
Piura
PERU
Madeira
Marabá
Imperatriz
Teresina
Natal
Chiclayo
Trujillo
Chimbote
Porto Velho
Xingu
Tocantins
Juazeiro do Norte
João Pessoa
Recife
Petrolina
Juazeiro
Rio Branco
Tapajós
BRAZIL
Maceió
Cerro de Pasco
Cobija
Guajará-Mirim
Araguaia
Aracaju
Callao
Huancayo
Feira de Santana
Salvador
Lima
Cusco
Ica
BOLIVIA
Cuiabá
Brasília
São Francisco
Itabuna
Puno
Anápolis
Vitória da Conquista
Arequipa
La Paz
Montes Claros
Tacna
Oruro
Santa Cruz de Sierra
Arica
Corumbá
Sucre
Potosí
Campo Grande
Uberlândia
Iquique
Ribeirão Preto
Belo Horizonte
Vitória
Ponta Porã
Campos
CHILE
PARAGUAY
Campinas
São Paulo
Rio de Janeiro
Santos
Antofagasta
Asunción
Salta
Paraná
Cascavel
Curitiba
Joinville
Isla San Ambrosio (Chil.)
Isla San Felix (Chil.)
San Miguel de Tucumán
Resistencia
Santiago del Estero
Corrientes
Florianópolis
Santa Maria
La Serena
Porto Alegre
San Juan
Córdoba
Riviera
Bagé
Santa Fe
Viña del Mar
Mendoza
Rio Grande
Archipiélago Juan-Fernandez (Chil.)
Valparaíso
Santiago
Rosario
URUGUAY
Buenos Aires
Montevideo
La Plata
Talca
Chillán
ARGENTINA
Tandil
Concepción
Mar del Plata
Temuco
Bahía Blanca
Punta Alta
Valdivia
Viedma
Puerto Montt
Esquel
Trelew
Puerto Aisén
Comodoro Rivadavia
Puerto Deseado
Puerto Santa Cruz
Rio Gallegos
Stanley
Falkland Is. (U.K.)
Punta Arenas
Tierra del Fuego
Cape Horn
South Georgia (U.K.)

EUROPE
0
500
1000
1500 km
ICELAND
Reykjavík
Akureyri
Seyðisfjördur
Faeroe Is.
(Dan.)
Shetland Is.
Orkney Is.
ATLANTIC
OCEAN
NORWEGIAN
SEA
NORTH
SEA
BARENTS
SEA
WHITE
SEA
BALTIC
SEA
MEDITERRANEAN SEA
BLACK SEA
AEGEAN
SEA
CASPIAN
SEA
Hammerfest
Murmansk
Kiruna
Bodø
Rovaniemi
Oulu
Archangel'sk
Onega
Sev. Dvina
Vorkuta
Salechard
Nar'jan-Mar
Ber'ozovo
Ob'
Surgut
Uchta
Serov
Syktyvkar
Berezniki
T'umen'
SWEDEN
FINLAND
NORWAY
RUSSIA
Trondheim
Umeå
Sundsvall
Petrozavodsk
Konoša
Perm'
Nižnij Tagil
Kirov
Jekaterinburg
Tampere
Gävle
Bergen
Oslo
Uppsala
Helsinki
Sankt-Peterburg
Vologda
Iževsk
Ufa
Stavanger
Stockholm
Tallinn
Novgorod
Jaroslavl'
Volga
Kazan'
Magnitogorsk
ESTONIA
Ivanovo
Nižnij Novgorod
Glasgow
Edinburgh
Ålborg
Göteborg
Pskov
Orsk
Belfast
IRELAND
Dublin
DENMARK
København
Riga
LATVIA
Velikije Luki
Moskva
Saransk
Samara
Orenburg
Akt'ubinsk
UNITED
KINGDOM
Cork
LITHUANIA
Vicebsk
Smolensk
Tula
Penza
Ural'sk
KAZAKHSTAN
Kaliningrad
Vilnius
Tambov
Saratov
Ural
Cardiff
NETHERLANDS
Hamburg
Gdańsk
Olsztyn
Minsk
Br'ansk
Bristol
London
Amsterdam
Elbe
Szczecin
Berlin
POLAND
Warszawa
BELARUS
Voronež
Plymouth
Poznań
Kursk
Don
Bruxelles
GERMANY
Köln
Wisła
Atyrau
Brest
BELG.
LUX.
Frankfurt
Wrocław
Lublin
Rivne
Kyyiv
Dnieper
Kharkiv
Volgograd
Paris
Le Mans
Rhein
Praha
Kraków
L'viv
UKRAINE
Astrachan'
Nantes
Tours
Nancy
Stuttgart
Donau
CZECH REP.
Vinnytsya
Dnipropetrovs'k
Donets'k
Fort-Ševčenko
Aktau
La Rochelle
FRANCE
München
Wien
Bratislava
SLOVAKIA
Bern
AUSTRIA
Budapest
MOLD.
Stavropol'
SWITZ.
Rhône
Lyon
HUNGARY
ROMANIA
Chisinău
Odesa
Krasnodar
Groznyj
Santiago de
Compostela
Bordeaux
Milano
SLOV.
Bilbao
Toulouse
Venezia
Ljubljana
Zagreb
VOJVODINA
Braşov
Simferopol'
Sevastopol'
Porto
Valladolid
Genova
Novi Sad
Bucuresti
Baki
Tbilisi
Marseille
CROATIA
BOSNIA
HERZ.
Beograd
Dunărea
Constanţa
GEORGIA
AZERBAIJAN
PORTUGAL
Monaco
Sarajevo
SERBIA
ARMENIA
Madrid
Barcelona
Firenze
Priština
BULGARIA
Varna
Jerevan
Lisboa
SPAIN
Corse
Roma
Podgorica
MONTENEGRO
KOSOVO
Sofija
Skopje
Samsun
Trabzon
Erzurum
ITALY
MACE.
Istanbul
TURKEY
Tabrīz
Sevilla
València
Palma
Alacant
Sardegna
Napoli
Bari
Tiranë
ALBANIA
Thessaloniki
Ankara
Bursa
Kayseri
Malatya
Málaga
Granada
Cagliari
GREECE
Hamadān
Tétouan
Palermo
Messina
Izmir
Konya
Kirkūk
Al-Mawşil
Sicilia
Catania
Pátrai
Athínai
Denizli
Adana
Halab
Rabat
Fès
Wahran
El Djazaïr
Qacentina
Tunis
Antalya
IRAQ
Tigris
MOROCCO
ALGERIA
TUNISIA
Malta
Kypros
SYRIA
Euphrates
Kriti

ASIA
0 500 1000 1500 km
(Norw.)
Zeml'a Franca-Iosifa
Severnaja Zeml'a
Novosibirskije Ostrova
BERING SEA
NORWAY
SWEDEN
FINLAND
BARENTS SEA
Novaja Zeml'a
KARA SEA
LAPTEV SEA
Murmansk
Tiksi
Verchojansk
Kamčatka
Petropavlovsk-Kamčatskij
Magadan
Archangel'sk
Vorkuta
Noril'sk
Ochotsk
SEA OF OKHOTSK
Severnaja Dvina
Volga
Salechard
Ob'
Jakutsk
Lena
Aldan
RUSSIA
Jenisej
Kirov
Surgut
Ocha
Nikolajevsk-na-Amure
Ostrov Sachalin
Kazan'
Perm'
Komsomol'sk-na-Amure
Jekaterinburg
Angara
Amur
Južno-Sachalinsk
Samara
Čel'abinsk
Bajkal
Blagoveščensk
Chabarovsk
Orenburg
Magnitogorsk
Omsk
Tomsk
Krasnojarsk
Sapporo
Ural'sk
Novosibirsk
Čita
Hakodate
Novokuzneck
Irkutsk
Ulan-Ude
Astana
Qiqihar Tsitsihar
Atyrau
Irtysh
Harbin
Vladivostok
KAZAKHSTAN
Kyzyl
Sendai
Karaganda
Semipalatinsk
Changchun
Jilin
Aral'skoe Ozero
Niigata
JAPAN
Ulaanbaatar
Tōkyō
Shenyang
NORTH KOREA
Balchaš
Yokohama
UZBEKISTAN
Ozero Balchaš
MONGOLIA
Anshan
P'yŏngyang
Kyōto
Ōsaka
Urgenč
Almaty
Dalian
Sŏul
Hiroshima
Yining
Ürümqi
Biškek
Baotou
Beijing
TURKMENISTAN
Taškent
Hami
SOUTH KOREA
Pusan
KYRGYZSTAN
Aschabad
Qingdao
Nagasaki
Taiyuan
EAST CHINA SEA
Huang
Kashi
Dušanbe
Mashhad
TAJIKISTAN
Shache
Xining
Zhengzhou
IRAN
CHINA
Lanzhou
Herāt
Kābol
Nanjing
Shanghai
Nansei-Shotō
AFGHANISTAN
Wuhan
Islāmābād
Indus
Qandahār
Wenzhou
Chang
Chengdu
Quetta
Changsha
Fuzhou
Multān
Chandigarh
Brahmaputra
PAKISTAN
Chongqing
Hengyang
T'aipei
Lhasa
Sukkur
Delhi
NEPAL
Gangā
Kāthmāndāu
TAIWAN
Guiyang
BHUTAN
Kaohsiung
Jaipur
Mekong
Karāchi
Lucknow
Kunming
Nanning
Xianggang (Hong Kong)
Allahābād
Vārānasi
BANGLADESH
Ahmadābād
Ha Noi
Dhaka
Jabalpur
Kolkata
Mandalay
Haikou
LAOS
INDIA
MYANMAR (BURMA)
Nāgpur
Quezon City
Cuttack
Viangchan
Mumbai
Manila
Pune
Chiang Mai
SOUTH CHINA SEA
Vishākhapatnam
Da Nang
Solāpur
Hyderābād
PHILIPPINES
THAILAND
Yangon
ARABIAN SEA
Belgaum
VIETNAM
Cebu
Qui Nhon
BAY OF BENGAL
Krung Thep (Bangkok)
CAMBODIA
Bangalore
Davao
Phnum Pénh
Chennai
Zamboanga
Thanh-pho Ho Chi Minh (Saigon)
Coimbatore
Andaman Islands (Ind.)
GULF OF THAILAND
Madurai
BRUNEI
Bandar Seri Begawan
Manado
SRI LANKA
Colombo
MALAYSIA
Galle
George Town
MALAYSIA
Borneo
MALDIVES
Male
Medan
Kuching
Kuala Lumpur
Samarinda
Sulawesi
Singapore
Pontianak
Sumatera
INDIAN OCEAN
INDONESIA
Banjarmasin
Padang
Ujungpandang
INDONESIA
Semarang
Surabaya
Jakarta
Jawa
Yogyakarta

AFRICA
0 500 1000 1500 km
ATLANTIC OCEAN
INDIAN OCEAN
MEDITERRANEAN SEA
BLACK SEA
CASPIAN SEA
RED SEA
GULF OF GUINEA
PORTUGAL
SPAIN
ITALY
GREECE
TURKEY
SYRIA
IRAQ
IRAN
LEBANON
ISRAEL
JORDAN
SAUDI ARABIA
U.A.E.
OMAN
YEMEN
MOROCCO
ALGERIA
TUNISIA
LIBYA
EGYPT
WESTERN SAHARA
MAURITANIA
MALI
NIGER
CHAD
SUDAN
ERITREA
ETHIOPIA
SOMALIA
SENEGAL
GUINEA
SIERRA LEONE
LIBERIA
IVORY COAST
GHANA
TOGO
BENIN
BURKINA FASO
NIGERIA
CAMEROON
CENTRAL AFRICAN REPUBLIC
EQUAT. GUINEA
GABON
CONGO
DEMOCRATIC REPUBLIC OF THE CONGO
UGANDA
KENYA
RWANDA
BURUNDI
TANZANIA
SEYCHELLES
COMOROS
MALAWI
ZAMBIA
ANGOLA
ZIMBABWE
MOZAMBIQUE
MADAGASCAR
MAURITIUS
NAMIBIA
BOTSWANA
SWAZILAND
LESOTHO
SOUTH AFRICA
Açores (Port.)
Madeira (Port.)
Islas Canarias (Esp.)
Ascension (U.K.)
St. Helena (U.K.)
Tristan da Cunha (U.K.)
Suqutrā (Yem.)
Réunion (Fra.)
Príncipe
São Tomé
Cape of Good Hope
Lisboa
Madrid
Roma
Athínai
Ankara
Izmir
Samsun
Tabrīz
Aśchabad
Tehrān
Kirkūk
Baghdād
Esfahān
Abādān
Al-Kuwayt
Bayrūt
Dimashq
'Ammān
Yerushalayim
Al-Hufūf
Ar-Riyāḍ
Dubayy
Al Madīnah
Makkah
San'ā'
'Adan
Tigris
Euphrates
Nile
Niger
Congo
Kasai
Zambezi
Tchad
Lake Viktoria
Lake Tanganyika
Lake Nyasa
El Djazaïr
Tunis
Annaba
Wahran
Rabat
Fès
Casablanca
Marrakech
Touggourt
Ghardaïa
Béchar
Tarābulus
Banghāzī
Al-Baydā'
Al-Iskandarīyah
Al-Qāhirah
Asyūt
Qinā
Aswān
Dirj
Amal
Sabhā
Ghāt
Reggane
In Salah
Tamenghest
El Aaiún
Nouadhibou
Nouakchott
Araouane
Tombouctou
Dakar
Bamako
Ouagadougou
Niamey
Zinder
Conakry
Monrovia
Abidjan
Accra
Lomé
Ibadan
Lagos
Abuja
Kano
Maiduguri
N'Djamena
Sarh
Bangui
Malabo
Yaoundé
Libreville
Brazzaville
Kinshasa
Būr Sūdān
Umm Durmān
Al-Khartūm
Al-Fāshir
Nyala
Al-Ubayyid
Wāw
Asmera
Djibouti
Dire Dawa
Adis Abeba
Muqdisho
Kismaayo
Buta
Kisangani
Kampala
Nairobi
Mombasa
Tanga
Zanzibar
Dar es Salaam
Dodoma
Viktoria
Moroni
Antsiranana
Nacala
Mahajanga
Antananarivo
Fianarantsoa
Port Louis
Kananga
Kamina
Luanda
Lobito
Huambo
Likasi
Lubumbashi
Ndola
Lusaka
Blantyre
Nampula
Livingstone
Harare
Bulawayo
Beira
Walvis Bay
Windhoek
Gaborone
Pretoria
Johannesburg
Xai-Xai
Maputo
Bloemfontein
Durban
East London
Port Elizabeth
Cape Town

AUSTRALIA & OCEANIA
0 500 1000 1500 2000 km
PACIFIC OCEAN
INDIAN OCEAN
SOUTHERN OCEAN
CHINA
SOUTH KOREA
JAPAN
U.S.
MIDWAY ISLANDS (U.S.)
HAWAIIAN ISLANDS (U.S.)
NORTHERN MARIANA ISLANDS (U.S.)
PHILIPPINES
GUAM (U.S)
MARSHALL ISLANDS (U.S.)
FEDERATED STATES OF MICRONESIA
PALAU (U.S.)
MALAYSIA
VIETNAM
INDONESIA
PAPUA NEW GUINEA
NAURU
KIRIBATI
TUVALU
SOLOMON ISLANDS
EAST TIMOR
AMERICAN SAMOA (U.S.)
SAMOA
FRENCH POLYNESIA (Fr.)
VANUATU
FIJI
TONGA
NEW CALEDONIA (Fr.)
COOK IS. (N.Z.)
PITCAIRN IS. (U.K.)
AUSTRALIA
NEW ZEALAND
Xi'an
Sŏul
Tōkyō
Hiroshima
Ōsaka
Fukuoka
Nanjing
Chongqing
Wuhan
Shanghai
Wenzhou
Fuzhou
Xiamen
T'aipei
Xianggang (Hong Kong)
Ha Noi
Haikou
Hainan
Nansei-Shotō (Jap.)
Ogasawara Is. (Jap.)
Minamitori-shima (Jap.)
Laoag
Olongapo
Manila
Quezon City
Ho Chi Minh (Saigon)
Iloilo
Cebu
Palawan
Mindanao
Bandar Seri Begawan
Kuching
Samarinda
Borneo
Manado
Ternate
Sulawesi
Seram
Banjarmasin
Jakarta
Jawa
Bali
Sumba
Timor
Tanimbar
New Guinea
Jayapura
Lae
Port Moresby
New Britain
Bougainville
Santa Isabel
Malaita
Honiara
San Cristobal
Saipan
Yap Is.
Chuuk Is.
Caroline Islands
Melanesia
Enewetak
Bikini
Kosrae
Tarawa
Banaba
Wake Island (U.S.)
Johnston Island (U.S.)
Niihau
Kauai
Oahu
Honolulu
Maui
Hawaii
San Francisco
Los Angeles
San Diego
Isla Guadalupe (Mex.)
Palmyra Atoll (U.S.)
Howland Is. (U.S.)
Baker Is. (U.S.)
Christmas Island
Phoenix Is.
Funafuti
Apia
Pago Pago
Suwarrow Is.
Bora Bora
Papeete
Tahiti
Îles Tuamotu
Îles Australes
Santa Cruz Is.
Port Vila
Éfaté
Suva
Nuku'alofa
Îles Loyauté
Nouméa
Arafura Sea
Coral Sea
Tasman Sea
Darwin
Wyndham
Birdum
Karumba
Cooktown
Cairns
Derby
Broome
Halls Creek
Townsville
Mackay
Mount Isa
Dajarra
Port Hedland
Marble Bar
Rockhampton
Alice Springs
Carnarvon
Quilpie
Wiluna
Oodnadatta
Brisbane
Southport
Norfolk Island
Mullewa
Geraldton
Kalgoorlie-Boulder
Eucla
Port Augusta
Broken Hill
Lord Howe Island
Perth
Merredin
Penong
Newcastle
Sydney
Bunbury
Esperance
Adelaide
Albury
Canberra
Albany
Ballarat
Melbourne
Tasmania
Launceston
Hobart
North Island
Auckland
New Plymouth
Napier
Wellington
South Island
Christchurch
Dunedin
Invercargill
Chatham Islands

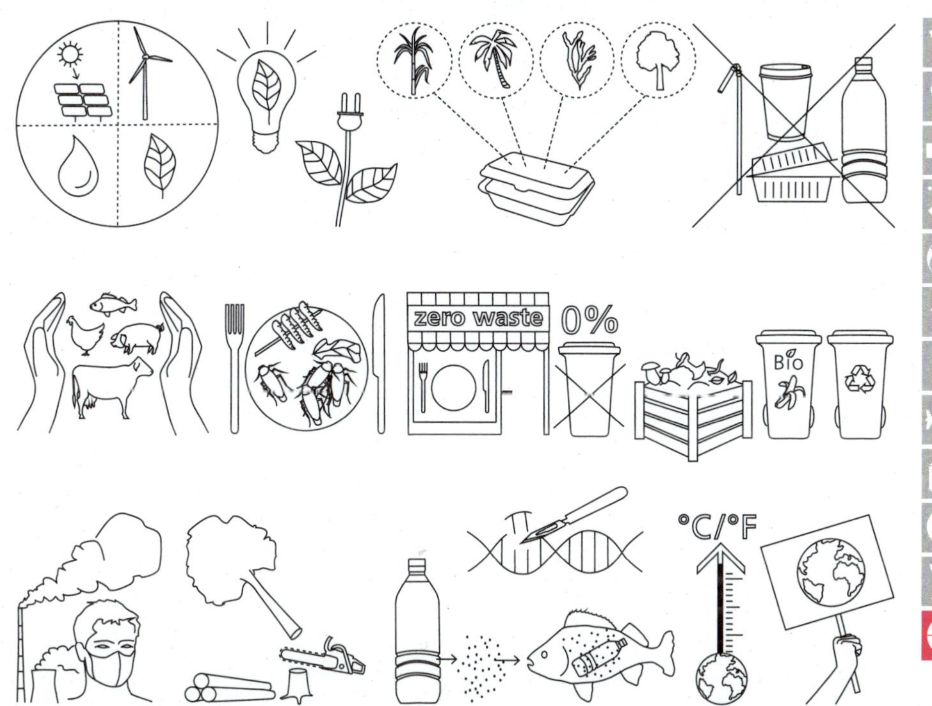
zero waste
0%
Bio
°C/°F